The Environment

Using Nonfiction to Promote Literacy Across the Curriculum

by Doris Roettger

Fearon Teacher Aids

A Paramount Communications Company

Teacher Consultants

Dawn Bassett
Des Moines, Iowa

Andrea Cressey
Altoona, Iowa

Merrilyn Goepel
Altoona, Iowa

Editorial Director: Virginia L. Murphy

Editor: Virginia Massey Bell

Copyeditor: Kristin Eclov

Illustration: Anita Nelson

Design: Terry McGrath

Cover Design: Lucyna Green

ISBN 0-86653-939-5

Printed in the United States of America

1. 9 8 7 6 5 4 3 2 1

A Note from the Author

*S*tudents have a natural curiosity about the world in which they live. They are intensely interested in learning about real things, real places, and real people. They also enjoy and learn from hands-on experiences. Nonfiction books and magazines provide opportunities for students to explore their interests and extend their base of knowledge.

Reading nonfiction materials is different from reading fiction. To be effective readers, students need to learn how to locate the information they want to answer their questions. They also need to learn to think about and evaluate the accuracy of the information presented. Finally, they need opportunities to learn the relationship between what they read and the activities in which they apply their new knowledge.

You, as the teacher, can provide opportunities for students to learn from their observations, their reading, and their writing in an integrated language-arts approach across the curriculum.

Modeling thinking strategies and then providing practice across the curriculum will help students become observers and explorers of their world, plus effective users of literacy skills. Encouraging students to extend and demonstrate their understanding through a variety of communication areas—speaking, reading, drama, writing, listening, and art—is also very valuable.

The suggestions in this guide are action-oriented and designed to involve students in the thinking process. The activities do not relate to any one single book. Instead, the strategies and activities are designed to be used with any of the books suggested in the bibliography or with books found in your own media center. The suggested interdisciplinary activities can also be used across grade levels.

Each lesson begins by reading a nonfiction book, book chapter, or magazine article to the class that relates to the follow-up activities you select. During the activity phase and at other class times, students are encouraged to return to the nonfiction selections available in the classroom to find answers to their questions, compare and verify their observations, and add new information to their current knowledge base.

The individual theme units are designed to be used for any length of time from a few days to a month or more, depending on the needs and interests of your students.

Suggested goals for this unit are provided near the beginning of this guide on page 16. The webs on pages 7–9 give you an overview of the areas in which activities are provided.

On each page of this guide, there is space for you to write reflective notes as well as ideas that you want to remember for future teaching. This guide is designed to be a rich resource from which you make the decisions and then select the learning experiences that will be the most appropriate for your students.

Doris Roettger

Contents

Literacy Skills

*T*he following literacy skills are addressed in *The Environment* theme guide.

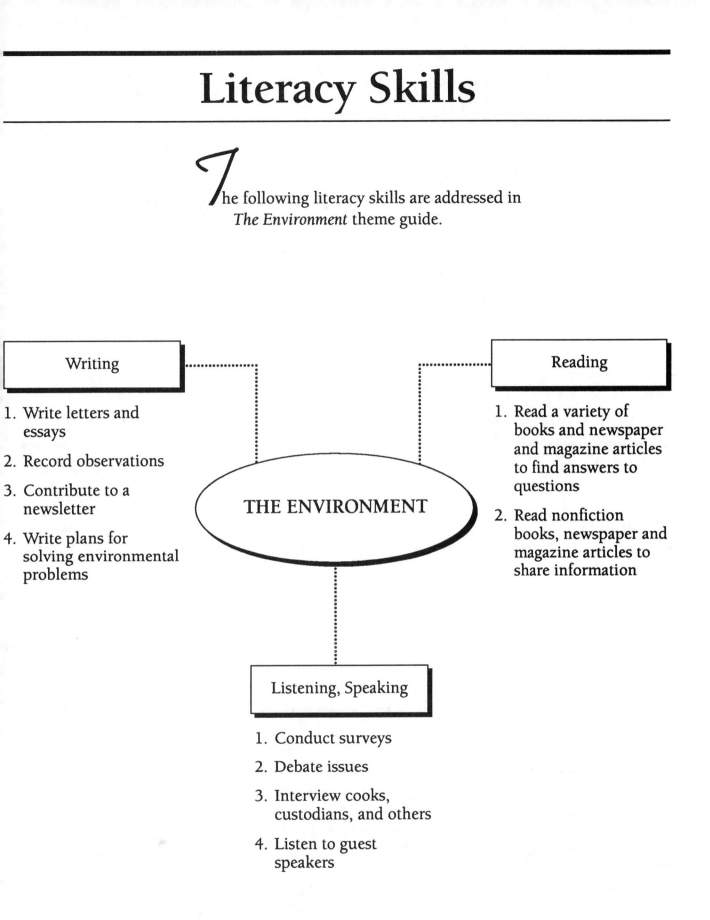

Writing

1. Write letters and essays

2. Record observations

3. Contribute to a newsletter

4. Write plans for solving environmental problems

THE ENVIRONMENT

Reading

1. Read a variety of books and newspaper and magazine articles to find answers to questions

2. Read nonfiction books, newspaper and magazine articles to share information

Listening, Speaking

1. Conduct surveys

2. Debate issues

3. Interview cooks, custodians, and others

4. Listen to guest speakers

Integrated Curriculum

The following interdisciplinary skills are addressed in The Environment theme guide.

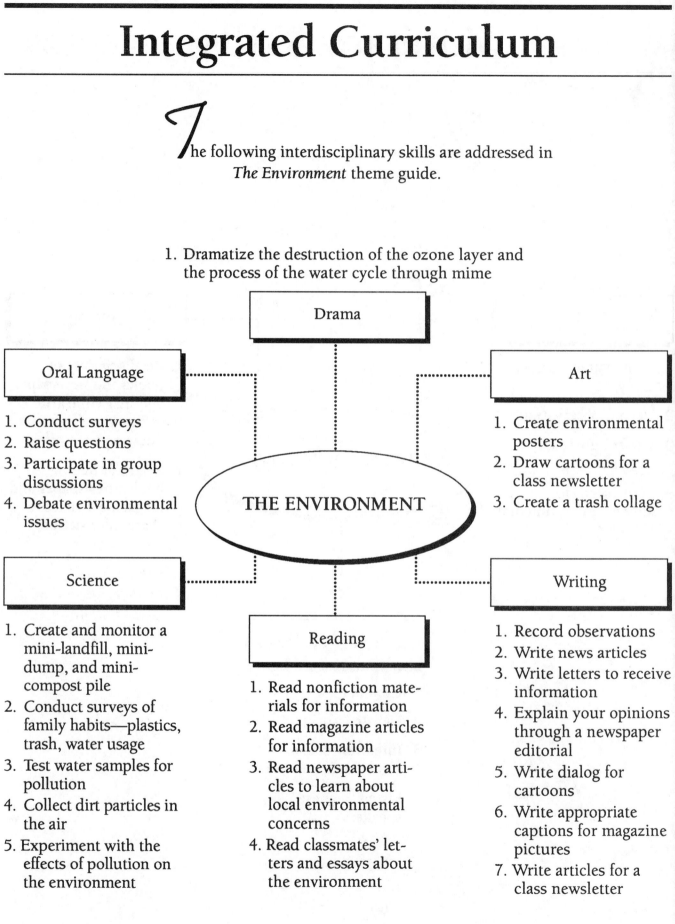

1. Dramatize the destruction of the ozone layer and the process of the water cycle through mime

Drama

Oral Language

1. Conduct surveys
2. Raise questions
3. Participate in group discussions
4. Debate environmental issues

Art

1. Create environmental posters
2. Draw cartoons for a class newsletter
3. Create a trash collage

THE ENVIRONMENT

Science

1. Create and monitor a mini-landfill, mini-dump, and mini-compost pile
2. Conduct surveys of family habits—plastics, trash, water usage
3. Test water samples for pollution
4. Collect dirt particles in the air
5. Experiment with the effects of pollution on the environment

Reading

1. Read nonfiction materials for information
2. Read magazine articles for information
3. Read newspaper articles to learn about local environmental concerns
4. Read classmates' letters and essays about the environment

Writing

1. Record observations
2. Write news articles
3. Write letters to receive information
4. Explain your opinions through a newspaper editorial
5. Write dialog for cartoons
6. Write appropriate captions for magazine pictures
7. Write articles for a class newsletter

Learning and Working Strategies

$\mathcal{T}$he following learning and working strategies are addressed in *The Environment* theme guide.

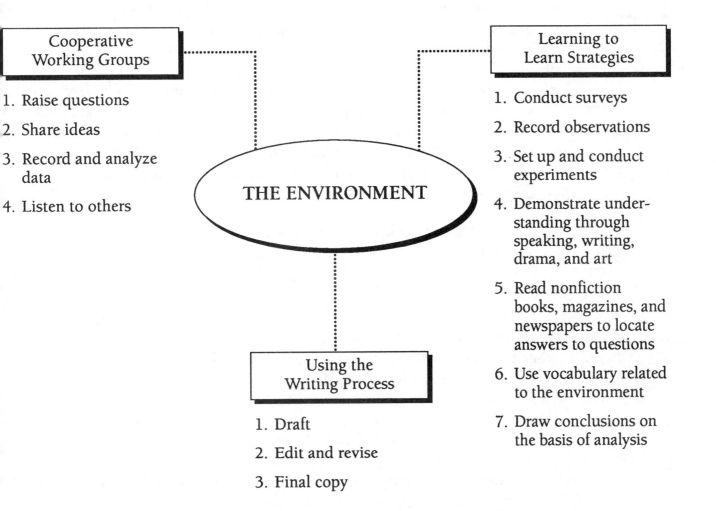

Cooperative Working Groups

1. Raise questions

2. Share ideas

3. Record and analyze data

4. Listen to others

THE ENVIRONMENT

Learning to Learn Strategies

1. Conduct surveys

2. Record observations

3. Set up and conduct experiments

4. Demonstrate understanding through speaking, writing, drama, and art

5. Read nonfiction books, magazines, and newspapers to locate answers to questions

6. Use vocabulary related to the environment

7. Draw conclusions on the basis of analysis

Using the Writing Process

1. Draft

2. Edit and revise

3. Final copy

About the Environment

*T*he environment is basically the world—everything on and around it. This includes the sky, the earth, the oceans, the people, all other living species— as well as objects created by human beings. In the last few years, the term *environment* has come to mean the natural world in which we live. In this unit, students will learn about the impact human beings have on the natural environment.

Our planet is made up of air, water, many plants, and a variety of animals. If we endanger any one of these important elements, the others are hurt as well. For example, the rainforests are being cut down at an alarming rate of approximately 100 acres per minute, leaving hundreds of species without habitats, as well as decreasing the amount of oxygen produced by the trees.

Human beings have the capacity to change the earth. We can build structures, move land, create lakes, change the course of rivers, cut down trees, burn fossil fuels, and toss away what we don't want. Over the last one hundred years, the Earth has changed a great deal due to inventions, such as automobiles, airplanes, factories, and so on. Progress has also brought with it many problems that need to be controlled or prevented—the greenhouse effect, air and water pollution, and rainforest destruction. We need to take an active role in the protection of our environment to ensure a healthy place to live for future generations.

Pollution is found all over the world. It affects rivers, oceans, air, and soil. Pollutants can be carried from one country to another by the wind or in ocean currents. Any form of pollution hurts the environment and is hard to stop once it's started. For example, one gallon of gasoline accidentally spilled on the ground can pollute up to 750,000 gallons of groundwater. We are all responsible for pollution because of the cars we drive, the foods we eat, and the energy we use. Therefore, each of us needs to help find ways to protect the environment.

There are many organizations and publications with additional information on this topic for you and your students. Addresses and telephone numbers are available in your library or local telephone directory. Some are listed here for your convenience.

For information about America's Clean Water Act and important facts about water and the amount of water needed for life's activities, contact:

America's Clean Water Foundation
750 First Street, NE Suite 911
Washington DC 20002
202-898-0902

Free educational materials on the issue of plastic recycling and plastics in waste are available from:

Partnership for Plastics Progress
PPP Education Program
1275 K Street NW, Suite 400
Washington, DC 20005
1-800-2-HELP-90

For information on Earth Day, write:

Earth Day
Box AA
Stanford University
Stanford, CA 99305

For information on environmental conservation, call or write:

U.S. Environmental Protection Agency
Office of Communications and Public Affairs
401 M St. SW, PM211B
Washington, DC 20460
202-382-2080

Kids for Saving Earth
P.O. Box 47247
Plymouth, MN 55447-0247
612-525-0002

Suggested Reading Selections

A variety of nonfiction and fiction selections for the intermediate grades is suggested for use with this theme unit. You will probably want to assemble a collection of materials ahead of time. Or, you may wish to have the students help collect several titles from the library as a group activity. The number and type of selections you and the students read will depend on the length of time you devote to this unit, as well as the availability of the titles.

Nonfiction Books

Environmental Awareness: Acid Rain by Mary Ellen Snodgrass. Marco, FL: Bancroft-Sage Publishing, Inc., 1991. Explains the effects of acid rain on plants, buildings, wildlife and on human life. Briefly describes acids and bases and how to test for them. Suggests ways industries, communities, and individuals can reduce the amount of acid rain. Lots of photographs.

Environmental Awareness: Air Pollution by Mary Ellen Snodgrass. Marco, FL: Bancroft-Sage Publishing, Inc., 1991. Explores pollution from smoke, industries, motor vehicles, acid rain, from farms and indoors. Suggests ways air can become cleaner. Promotes the individual's role in protecting the air. Lots of photographs.

Environmental Awareness: Solid Waste by Mary Ellen Snodgrass. Marco, FL: Bancroft-Sage Publishing, Inc., 1991. Industries, farms, the military, and individuals are common causes of solid waste. Solid waste can be managed through recycling centers, composting, landfills, and incinerators. Suggests ways individuals can reduce waste through reducing and recycling.

Environmental Awareness: Water Pollution by Mary Ellen Snodgrass. Marco, FL: Bancroft-Sage Publishing, Inc., 1991. Describes sources of water, how pollution threatens our water supply, and ways that our water supply can be protected. Suggests ways that individuals can help in keeping water clean.

Environmental Diseases by Madelyn Klein Anderson. New York, NY: Franklin Watts, 1987. The first half of the book discusses a person's internal environment, one's genes and one's resistance, immunity and causes for illness. The last three chapters describe how chemicals reach both surface and ground water, the air, and landfills. Names and briefly describes a variety of chemicals and their effects on health.

50 Simple Things Kids Can Do to Save the Earth by EarthWorks Group. Kansas City, MO: Andrews and McMeel, 1990. Explains how students can take an active role in protecting the planet.

Good Planets Are Hard to Find by Roma Dehr and Ronald Bazar. Buffalo, NY: Firefly Books Limited, 1990. An environmental information guide, dictionary, and action book for children and adults.

Groundwater by Mary Hoff and Mary M. Rodgers. Minneapolis, MN: Lerner Publications Co., 1991. Informs the reader of the importance of water for all forms of life. Good description of where groundwater is located, how water is pumped out of the ground, and how it can be endangered. Includes ways individuals can ensure that groundwater stays clean. Beautiful photographs.

The Kids' Environment Book by Anne Pedersen. Santa Fe, NM: John Muir Publications, 1991. Notes that while there is a lot of information about the environment, some of it is confusing and some of it is wrong. Presents a balanced approach to the discussion of concerns about air and water. Looks at how industry contributes both to our standard of living and to pollution problems. Presents the effects of the different types of energy. Includes a chapter on ways individuals can take responsibility for doing something good for the environment. Nice illustrations and photographs.

Pesticides by John Duggleby. New York, NY: Crestwood House, 1990. Defines pesticides as insecticides, rodenticides, fungicides, and herbicides. Briefly mentions the positive effects of each. Also explains negative effects of each. Short section on what individuals can do to reduce possible pesticide damage.

Pollution and Wildlife by Michael Bright. New York, NY: Gloucester Press, 1987. Explains the effects of pollution in fields on the insects and animals that are part of a food chain. Brief description of freshwater runoff, acid rain, and the effects of oil and other wastes in the ocean. Excellent illustrations.

Save the Earth: An Action Handbook for Kids by Betty Miles. New York, NY: Alfred Knopf, 1991. Long- and short-term projects for students related to the environment. Interesting facts also presented in a bulleted format.

Fiction Books

The Black Pearl by Scott O'Dell. New York, NY: Dell, 1977. A sixteen-year-old pearl diver discovers a magnificient black pearl. He then must face underwater danger in order to keep his valuable prize.

Brother Eagle, Sister Sky by Susan Jeffers. New York, NY: Dial Books, 1991. Describes the special relationship between the Native American, the Earth, and its creatures.

Call of the Wild by Jack London. New York, NY: Grosset & Dunlap, 1931. A dog is forcibly taken to Alaska where he eventually becomes the leader of a wolf pack.

I'm in Charge of Celebrations by Byrd Baylor. New York, NY: Charles Scribner's Sons, 1986. A celebration of the many wonders of the desert wilderness.

The Island of the Blue Dolphins by Scott O'Dell. New York, NY: Dell, 1987. A courageous story of the survival of a young girl stranded alone on an island for eighteen years.

Julie of the Wolves by Jean Craighead George. New York, NY: HarperCollins, 1972. A young Eskimo girl is befriended by a pack of Arctic wolves as she travels on foot across the frozen North slope of Alaska.

The Lorax by Dr. Seuss. New York: Random House, 1971. In verse, we look at one man's impact on the environment as he ignores the Lorax's wisdom to save the trees.

My Side of the Mountain by Jean Craighead George. New York, NY: Dutton, 1988. A young boy shares his experiences of living alone in the Catskill Mountains.

20,000 Leagues Under the Sea by Jules Verne. New York, NY: D. McKay Co., 1976. A 19th-century science fiction tale of the fascinating undersea world of Captain Nemo.

Magazines and Newspapers

Garbage—the Practical Journal for the Environment, 435 Ninth Street, Brooklyn, NY 11215-9937. Published six times a year. Numerous ads for environmental materials and equipment. Gives readers ideas about what is available, plus how individuals can become involved in environmental issues. Some feature articles may be more adult-oriented.

Kids for Saving Earth News, Kids for Saving Earth, P. O. Box 47247, Plymouth, MN 55447-0247. Published four times a year. Filled with articles and information about what kids are doing to help protect the Earth. Sponsored by the Kids for Saving Earth® club.

National Geographic World, National Geographic Society, 17 & M Street NW, Washington, DC 20036. Published monthly for children ages 8-13. General information on a variety topics concerning the natural world. Exceptional photography.

Teacher Reference

Keepers of the Earth by Michael J. Caduto and Joseph Bruchac. Golden, CO: Fulcrum, Inc., 1989. Excellent detailed information with suggested questions and activities on all topics related to the environment.

Going Green by John Elkington, Julia Hailes, Douglas Hill, and Joel Makover. New York, NY: Viking Penguin, 1990. A child's handbook to saving the planet. Explains the greenhouse effect and ways to recycle at home and at school.

Instructional Goals

*I*nstructional goals for this theme unit are provided here. Space is also provided so that you may fill in your own individual goals where appropriate as well. By the end of this theme unit, students should be able to:

1. Define the words *environment* and *pollution*.

2. Identify local environmental concerns from newspaper articles.

3. Conduct informational surveys at home and at school.

4. Create a mini-sanitary landfill, mini-dump, and mini-compost pile. Identify the differences between a landfill and a dump.

5. Test water samples from local lakes, ponds, streams, or rivers for acidity.

6. Write articles and draw cartoons for an environmental newsletter.

7. Identify recycling codes on the bottoms of plastic containers.

8. Identify possible causes of water pollution.

9. Work in small groups to create plans for clarifying water samples and cleaning up oil slicks.

10. Experiment with the effects of acid rain on the environment.

11. Identify the steps of the water cycle.

12. Demonstrate how the greenhouse effect works.

13. Test air for pollution and draw conclusions.

14. ....

15. ....

16. ....

17. ....

18. ....

19. ....

20. ....

Getting Started

Finding Out What Students Already Know and Raising Curiosity

*T*he following activities are designed to help launch *The Environment* theme unit. You may want to use all of the activities or only one or two, depending on the needs of your students. At the beginning of each lesson, reading a nonfiction book or magazine selection to the class serves as a motivator and helps students become more familiar with and involved in using nonfiction selections. You'll also want to provide plenty of opportunities for students to return to nonfiction selections independently during the activity phases and at other times during class periods as well.

1. Celebrating the Environment

a. Think of a place in your state that is a place of natural beauty. If possible, bring in several photographs and then discuss with the class this particular spot and what makes it so beautiful.

b. Suggest that the class celebrate the many beautiful spots around your state. Ask the students to bring in photographs of special places they have visited. Remind students to write their names on the backs of their photographs.

c. Create a bulletin board entitled "Celebrating Nature." Display the pictures brought in by the students.

d. Read the book *I'm in Charge of Celebrations* by Byrd Baylor. As a group, discuss the things in nature that she celebrates.

2. Graffiti Wall

a. Write "Graffiti Wall" across the top of a large sheet of butcher paper. Then divide the sheet into two sections. Write *environment* in one section and *pollution* in the other. Tape the paper on a wall or bulletin board where students have access to it.

b. Give students two sticky notes and ask the class to write or draw what they think each of the words means. Have students stick their definitions on the graffiti wall.

c. Hold a class meeting. First have students read the definitions for *environment* and *pollution* from a dictionary or glossary of one of the books from the suggested reading section. Ask students to read all the responses on the graffiti wall and then decide which ones best fit the dictionary definitions.

d. Ask students to classify the responses. This will help provide information about the type of knowledge students are bringing to the unit.

3. The Conflict Between Improving Our Way of Life and Pollution of the Environment

a. Have each student complete the "Our Way of Life Survey" found on page 61. Then hold a class discussion on how responses to certain items might affect the air, water, and land.

b. Hold a class meeting and ask the students to describe how our way of life has become easier than it was for people during the frontier days or some other time period before automobiles. Ask students to describe how the changes they have mentioned have affected the environment, the air we breathe, our water supply, and the land, including trees and plants.

c. Visit a new housing development, mall, or land that is being cleared for building construction. Take one or more pictures of the area. Look at the surrounding area to see what kinds of changes will need to be made to accommodate the new development, such as roads, water and sewage system, and so on. Where is this place? What used to be there? Who owns this land? How could the land in this area be reclaimed?

d. As a group, discuss changes that are for the better and changes that are for the worse.

4. Tapping into Local Environmental Concerns

a. Ask students to look through newspapers for several weeks before beginning this unit for articles pertaining to water, rivers, lakes, air, land, landfills, and pollution. Have the students bring the articles to class.

b. Have students read the newspaper articles and write down their responses to the local environmental problems. In a large group, ask students to share the information they found. Discuss the environmental problems and possible solutions. Record the students' responses on chart paper in order to refer to the problems and solutions throughout the unit.

5. Introducing Resource Materials

a. Introduce a variety of books, magazines, and newspapers that provide information about the environment and pollution. Ask students to generate a list of questions they'd like answered. Record the questions on chart paper for future reference.

b. Encourage students to identify the key words from their lists of questions. Have students use the indexes and glossaries in various resources to locate information about these key words.

c. Have students read aloud information addressing their particular questions. As a class, evaluate the information to determine whether it answers the questions.

6. Forming Research Teams

a. Explain to students that they will be participating in research activities that will help them better understand the air they breathe, the water they drink, and the land around where they live. They will be learning about the effects of pollution and what can be done about it.

b. Explain that as researchers students will:

raise questions about various aspects of the environment and pollution.

look for answers to their questions.

read for information.

help set up research projects.

take notes on what they observe.

study the information they find.

report their findings to their classmates, parents, and community members.

Real-Life Laboratory

Solid Waste—It's a Mess

*T*he activities in this section will heighten the students' awareness of solid waste in the environment. Select one or two books or articles on solid waste to share with the class before students begin an activity.

1. Important and Interesting Information to Know

NOTES

a. Write each of the following facts on cards and then post the cards around the room.

- Americans on the average throw out between 3.5 to 4 pounds of trash per person every day. This includes food garbage as well as paper, cardboard, and so on.

- Approximately one-third of the garbage Americans throw out is packaging that is thrown out immediately.

- Solid waste is unwanted material that is discarded by individuals, industries, and communities.

- As a society we tend to focus on the things we can see, such as trash and household chemicals, at the expense of invisible things, such as energy and water. It is important that everyone makes an effort to stop polluting.

b. Give students a copy of the survey "Kinds and Amounts of Trash at Home" found on page 62. If necessary, go over the directions to make sure students fully understand what they are being asked to do.

c. At the end of one week, students should return their completed survey forms. Help students compile the information onto a large chart-sized version of the survey.

d. Ask students to study the information they have collected about trash in their homes. Challenge students to add all the total weights recorded on the surveys together.

e. Explain that much of the newspaper, magazines, other paper, plastic, and glass can be recycled. Challenge the students to discover the differences recycling can make in the amount of trash accumulated each year, particularly in the United States.

2. Recycling Plastic

Explain that plastic recycling centers categorize plastic by numbers. Plastics with a #1 are easiest to recycle, a #7 is the most difficult. Encourage students to research the letter codes on the bottoms of the plastic containers, too, such as PETE or PET, HOPE, LDPE, PP, and PS. Have students record the recycling code from each plastic item they find at home. Encourage students to share this information with their families. As a class, compile the data collected from home and discuss the results. For information on plastic recycling, contact:

> Partnership for Plastic Progress
> PPP Education Program
> 1275 K Street NW, Suite 400
> Washington, DC 20005
> 1-800-2-HELP-90

3. Packaging

Explain that many items we purchase are heavily packaged. Ask students which kinds of products have the most elaborate packaging and how the packaging might be changed to be more environmentally friendly. Invite each student to choose one product and redesign the packaging. Display the packaging innovations around the classroom. Encourage students to write letters to product manufacturers asking them to use less packaging. Addresses of companies can be obtained from the reference librarian at the public libraries.

4. Finding Out What Happens to the Trash at School

Invite the custodian to talk with the students about what happens to the trash collected at school each day. Find out how much, if any, is recycled.

5. Where Does All the Garbage Go?

a. Visit a landfill in your community. Find out:

How long the landfill has been in existence.

How much garbage comes into the landfill each week.

What is done to help the garbage decompose.

How long before the landfill will be full.

What will be done when the landfill becomes full.

How is it decided where to put a landfill.

b. Invite a speaker from the solid waste management department and from a recycling center to come speak to the students about what is being done in your community and what the students, as individuals, can do to help stop pollution. Ask the speakers to explain the steps in recycling.

6. How Is a Dump Different from a Sanitary Landfill?

Explain to the students that they are going to make a box-size dump and a box-size sanitary landfill in the classroom and compare the two over several months.

a. Bring in two medium-sized plastic boxes. If you cannot find plastic boxes, use a cardboard box for the dump and a strong, clear plastic bag for the landfill.

b. Cover the bottoms of the two containers with soil or sand.

c. Collect items that are made by people, such as aluminum foil, glass, metal jar lids, and newspaper. List the objects and make a note about how they look at the beginning of the experiment. If possible, take a picture of the items.

d. In the landfill, bury the items in the soil or sand. Add more soil or sand so that the objects are completely covered. For the dump, just put the items on top of the soil.

e. Collect items that come from nature, such as apples, carrots, twigs, eggshells, and leaves. List the items and describe how they look at the beginning of the experiment. Again, if possible, take a picture of the items.

f. Bury half of the items in the landfill adding more soil or sand, if necessary. Place the other half of the items in the dump.

g. Sprinkle water on the landfill. Then close the container tightly and put it in an area where it will not be disturbed. If possible, put it outside next to the building.

h. Each week, open the landfill and sprinkle more water on the soil or sand. Be sure the top of the soil is always moist.

i. Every three weeks, empty the landfill into a big box. Look at each object. Be sure that students wear plastic disposable gloves when they check the decomposing objects. How have the objects changed? Also, check the items in the dump. How are they changing? Take pictures of both. Then put everything back into their containers and close them.

j. After four or five months, make a chart to show how each item in both the dump and the landfill have changed. Include any pictures that were taken during the project.

7. Posters

Encourage students to create posters showing problems with waste or ways to reduce, reuse, and recycle materials. Display the posters prominently in the school.

8. Composting

a. Inquire about the possibility of creating a compost pile on the school grounds. Explain that you and your class will be collecting food scraps, coffee grounds from the teachers' lounge, twigs, and grass clippings from around the school. Be sure to explain that the class will develop a plan for collecting the composting materials and that you will consult with the custodian about where the compost pile can be located.

b. Start with a layer of twigs, then add vegetable and fruit scraps, eggshells, and coffee grounds. Next, add a layer of grass clippings, and then a layer of soil. Continue alternating the different layers of materials. To speed up the composting process, add some manure to the pile. Make sure the pile stays moist. Continue adding layers until the pile is about two feet high and then cover the pile with plastic.

c. When the compost has turned into a rich mixture, have students spread it around plants, trees, and bushes on the school grounds.

9. What We Can Do to Reduce Pollution?

a. Hold a class meeting to talk about ways we, as individuals, can help reduce solid waste pollution. Introduce students to the recycle symbol. Ask students what it means.

b. Place the students into cooperative working groups of four or five students each. Ask the groups to list ways that each member can:

> reduce solid waste
>
> reuse items
>
> recycle items
>
> conserve energy

c. Have each group share one idea they've discussed in groups. Write the ideas on a large sheet of butcher paper and hang the paper where students can refer back to the list of suggestions at a later time. Encourage students to add to the list as they think of ideas and as they come across suggestions in the books and magazines that they read.

d. Ask students to look for products that use recycled paper, cardboard, and plastics. Invite students to bring in some of the items to display in the classroom. Hold a class meeting to share the names of items made from recycled materials.

10. Sharing Information from Books, Newspapers, and Magazines

a. Invite each student to write several questions about pollution and waste management on 5" x 7" index cards. Encourage students to find answers to their questions by looking through books, newspapers, and magazines for articles on pollution and waste management.

b. Hold frequent small group discussions for students to share information and discuss how this information answers some of their questions or gives them new ideas to think about. Display the question cards around the classroom. Encourage students to continue to research any unanswered questions.

11. Writing Letters for Information

Write to the Environmental Protection Agency for your region asking for your state's goals and methods to reduce solid waste. The address can be obtained from your community's solid waste agency listed in the yellow pages of your local phone book under Public Service Bureau of Environment Management.

Write to the Environmental Protection Agency in Washington, DC for information on states with the most effective methods of handling solid waste, such as curbside recycling programs. Challenge students to compare their state's solid waste management program with the most effective examples from around the country. For information, contact:

> U.S. Environmental Protection Agency
> Office of Communications and Public Affairs
> 401 M St. SW, PM211B
> Washington, DC 20460
> 202-382-2080

12. Letters of Inquiry

Write letters to students in other classes asking if they would participate in collecting, sorting, and monitoring the trash accumulated in their classrooms for one week. Ask the students to keep track of the specific items thrown away each day. Include an explanation for monitoring trash in the classroom and any interesting facts to convince the other students to participate in the project. At the end of the week, invite the other classes to share their information with your students.

13. Trash Collage

Invite students to create a collage using trash from materials they have collected.

14. Thank-You Letters

Have students write thank-you letters to all the people who participated in the class study of solid waste, such as students in participating classrooms, parents for assisting with the surveys, and guest speakers. Encourage students to include some of the information they learned from the various surveys and guest speakers. Create a simple bar graph to illustrate the information collected from the surveys, such as the most common types of plastics used in the home or the average amount of trash thrown out in one week, and include a copy with each thank-you letter.

15. Letters to Companies That Use Recycled Paper

After students have collected samples of products that have been recycled, suggest that they write to the customer relations departments of those companies complimenting them on their efforts to protect the environment. Addresses of the companies can be obtained from the reference librarians at public libraries.

16. Producing an Environmental Awareness Newsletter

a. As a group, list environmental topics for articles that would be of interest to parents and other students in the school, including:

the kinds of trash and garbage collected at school

the results of the packaging survey (see page 26)

the class dump and sanitary landfill project (see page 27)

b. Review how to write an informational article. The first paragraph should answer the questions who, what, when, where, why, and how. Each of the other paragraphs should give important and interesting details. Encourage peer editing. Invite students to draw cartoons on any of the topics.

c. Bring several editorials on the environment to class. Read the editorials aloud and help students determine each author's point of view. Invite students to write an editorial on a topic about which they feel very strongly and for which they have important facts and details. Encourage students to create editorial cartoons, too.

d. Ask for volunteers to help lay out the format for a newsletter. Send a copy of the newsletter to all the people the students worked with during this part of their environmental studies.

17. Trash Patrols

a. Invite students to form trash patrols to pick up trash on the school grounds.

b. Form patrols of four to six students, depending on the size of the school grounds. Set up a schedule for the patrols to be responsible for trash pickup.

c. Hold a meeting of all patrol members to discuss responsibilities and a schedule. Provide plastic disposable gloves for patrol members.

d. Members of the trash patrol might visit other classrooms to inform all students about what they are finding and to encourage students to throw things away in trash containers or classroom wastebaskets.

e. Plan a party or field trip as a reward for the patrol's hard work and dedication.

Water—Where It Is, How We Use It, Pollution, and What Can Be Done

The activities in this section will help students become aware of the water cycle, what pollutes and wastes water, and what they can do to help save this precious resource.

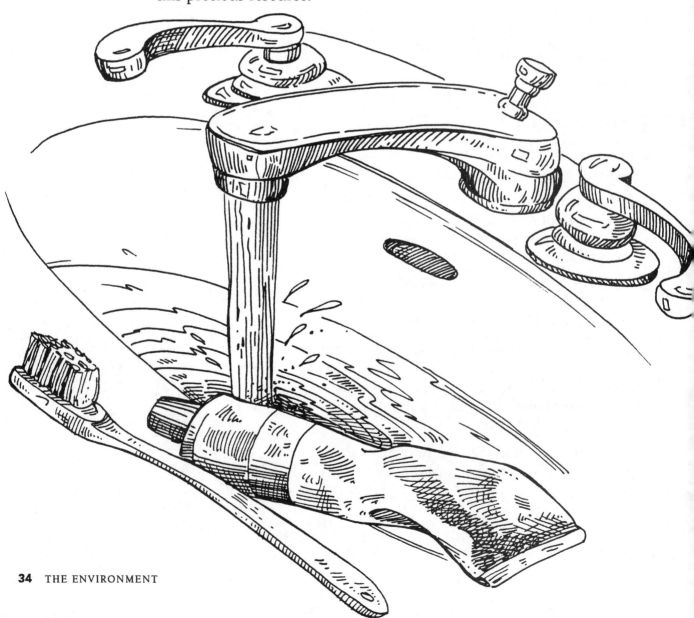

1. Important and Interesting Information to Know

NOTES

Write the following information on cards and then display the cards around the classroom.

- About 70% of the Earth is water.

- The amount of water in the world stays the same and is constantly circulating between bodies of water, the atmosphere, and the land.

- About 97% of the water on the Earth is in the oceans (which is salty) and only 3% of all water on Earth is fresh water.

- An average American uses 200 gallons of water a day.

- It takes 1400 gallons of water to process a meal consisting of 1/4 lb. hamburger, an order of fries, and a soft drink.

- Approximately 90% of the water that human beings can drink right now comes from underground. The Earth is like a sponge, anything that is poured or spilled on the ground can pollute the groundwater, such as pesticides, gasoline, household cleaners, and so on.

2. Visit Local Bodies of Water for Water Samples

NOTES

a. Using a local or county map, have students identify the location of some or all of the bodies of water in your area.

b. Take a field trip to several bodies of water in your area to take pictures of the environment and to collect three small samples of water at each site. Baby food jars with lids are good containers for collecting water samples. Label the jars with the source of the water sample. Use the procedure described in the activity "Testing the Water" on page 37 to examine the various water samples. If possible, take pictures of the trips for a class booklet on the environment.

c. In a notebook, have students write observations about the water area, such as whether the water was clear or cloudy or whether there were factories, homes, or farms nearby.

3. Expanding the Knowledge Base

a. Hold a class discussion on what the students have observed and learned about water so far. As a group, create a web of the information students know about water on a sheet of chart paper. Save the web for future reference.

b. Encourage students to raise questions about their observations and other aspects of water. List the questions on a large sheet of butcher paper or write each question on a separate sheet of paper. Display the questions in the classroom.

c. Encourage students to find answers to their questions through experiments, reading, and interviewing people knowledgeable about their water concerns. As students find answers to their questions, have them record the answers under the appropriate questions.

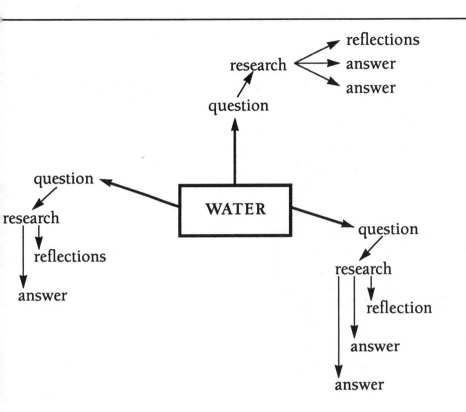

4. Testing the Water

a. You will need the following materials for testing water samples:

> samples of water from a nearby water site—pond, river, lake, and so on

> small, clean, empty containers, such as baby food jars

> coffee filters

> litmus test tabs

> color test strips (available at stores that sell tropical fish)

b. Test the cleanliness of the water.

1. Place a coffee filter over the mouth of a clean jar. Pull it tight and secure it with a rubber band.

2. Pour a water sample through the filter. Look at the filter to see if it is discolored. Look at any discoloration with a magnifying glass.

3. Label the filter and the filtered water sample.

4. Have students record their observations in their notebooks.

c. Test the acidity of the water.

1. Place a litmus tab in one sample of water from each location visited.

2. Determine whether the water is acid, alkaline, or neutral by comparing the tab to the color strip sample below.

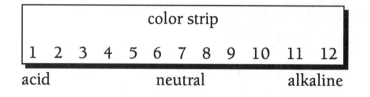

3. Ask students to jot their observations in their notebooks.

d. Call the community water treatment center or extension agent of a university to make arrangements to have the water samples tested for chemicals.

e. Hold a discussion about what the students have observed and raise new questions. Encourage students to reread the notes they took at each of the water sites. Did they jot down anything that would give them clues to the quality of the water? If the water is polluted, what might be the cause?

f. Have the students record their questions. Help students determine where they can find the answers to their questions. As a place to start, refer students to the books that are available in the classroom, school, or public library. Encourage students to look for articles in newspapers, as well.

5. Use of Water in the Community

Have a group of students write a letter to the local water utility to determine how much water is used in your community on an average day. In a year? Ask how homes and businesses are charged for the water they use. Share the responses with the class.

6. Research Teams Look for Causes of Water Pollution

If your class has found an area where the water is polluted, set up research teams to look for causes of the pollution. Ask your community water treatment center or a university extension to test the water samples to find out what pollutants are present. Encourage the team members to read, interview people, and make observations to locate information about the sources of water pollution. Hold frequent discussion sessions so students can share what they have learned.

a. Visit a nursery or plant center. Read the labels on the pesticide and insecticide containers. Were any of the chemicals listed on the containers in the water samples that were tested? If so, what are some of the possible ways that the chemicals could have gotten into the water?

b. Encourage students to enlist the help of family members to look for chemicals used in the home. Remind the students to record the information in their notebooks.

c. If farms are near the water site, write to fertilizer manufacturers or dealers asking for the names of the fertilizers most farmers use and the ingredients found in these fertilizers. The chemicals in the fertilizers, pesticides, and herbicides can contaminate water sources.

d. If factories are close to the water site, write to the environmental engineer of each company to ask what their source of energy is and how they are disposing of wastes. Before students write, if necessary, teach how to write a letter for information. To ensure a response, call your community's reference librarian for the correct address of each company.

e. As students gather information, provide time for them to talk about their research. Help students organize their information by constructing a web of what they already know.

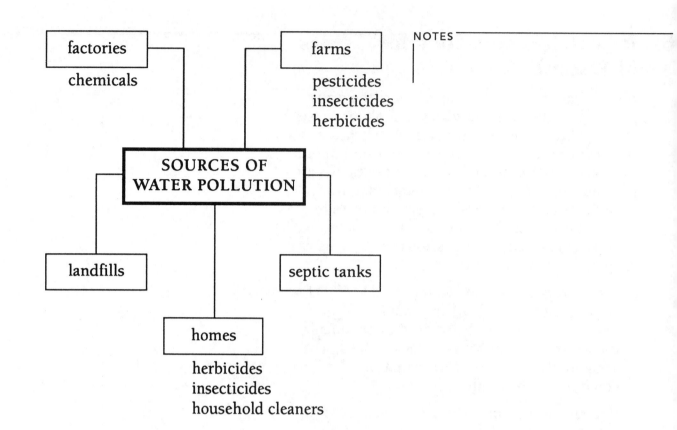

f. After students have reviewed the water pollution web, encourage them to raise new questions. Answers to these questions can be found during a visit to a sewage treatment plant, a water purification plant, and through reading materials from the bibliography.

7. Classroom Environmental Newsletter

Ask students to decide what they want to contribute to an environmental newsletter on water conservation. Encourage students to collect cartoons, news articles, reports of any surveys, and editorials to be included in the newsletter.

8. Visit a Sewage-Treatment Plant

NOTES

a. Ask students what they think happens to all the water that leaves their houses and what happens to rain when it runs into a storm sewer or into the ground.

b. Arrange for a visit to a sewage-treatment plant to learn what actually happens to water once it leaves homes or businesses. Have students attempt to draw pictures of the process. If a visit is not possible, invite a speaker from a sewage-treatment plant to come talk with the students. If possible, take pictures for a class booklet.

9. Visit a Water Purification Plant

a. First, explain to students that water that comes from groundwater may only require disinfection. If water comes from a river and comes in contact with recreational activities or potential sewage contamination, it will require more purification. Possibilities include the use of alum, water filtered through sand or charcoal, aeration, and the use of chlorine. Ask students if they know where their drinking water comes from and whether it's free of pollution.

b. Arrange for a tour of a water purification plant or invite someone from the plant to come talk with the students. Ask what process the area's drinking water undergoes for purification. Again, if possible, take pictures for a class booklet.

10. Experimenting to Clarify Water

a. Divide the class into cooperative working groups of four or five students. Give each team a bottle of water which contains some mud, small pebbles, sand, and a little food coloring. Provide funnels, coffee filters, small pieces of screen, cheesecloth, charcoal, and empty bottles.

b. Each team should write a plan of action for making the water clear and present it in exchange for the materials needed to conduct the experiment. If teams need additional materials, try to provide them. Explain to the students that clarity of water does not automatically mean the water is pure—impurities may still exist in clear water.

c. As teams make changes in their plans to purify the water, they should also modify their written plans. Each team should keep track of the amount of time it takes to clarify the water.

d. When the teams complete the water clarification project, hold a class meeting so students can compare the processes they went through and the amount of time it took for them to complete the task. Each team should show their bottle of water after completing the project. If possible, take pictures of this activity for a class booklet.

11. Cleaning Up Oil Slicks

a. Collect several newspaper and magazine articles about oil spills.

b. Give students a large glass pan with about two inches of water in the bottom. Pour a small amount of motor oil on top of the water. Put toy fish or a toy duck into the water. Explain that sometimes there are accidents where oil spills into rivers, lakes, and oceans by barges or tankers. Sometimes industries dump oil into our waters as well.

c. Have students read newspaper and magazine articles to determine what has been used to clean up oil spills. Give students the task of cleaning the oil from the water. Ask them to keep a log of everything they try.

d. Hold several discussions about the effects of oil spills on water, plants, and animals.

12. Miming the Water Cycle

a. Ask students to find an illustration of the water cycle in one of the resource books. As a group, trace the path of the water cycle.

b. Use mime to further students' understanding that the amount of water on Earth always stays the same and that it is always moving through evaporation from oceans, lakes, rivers, and ponds, or through rain, snow, hail, and sleet. Narrate the steps of the water cycle as the students mime the process.

Characters:

sun	clouds
lakes	oceans
rivers	trees
wind	shrubs

Directions:

1. Have the sun stand on a chair or counter so it can shine on the water and the plants.

2. Two or three clouds should stand in different locations, each with a large empty bucket.

3. Have the students acting out the characters of the ocean, the lakes, the rivers, the trees, and the shrubs scatter around the room with the clouds in the background. The ocean should have a large bucket filled with water. The lakes should have buckets which are not quite as full, rivers with less water, and the trees and shrubs with even less water. Each of these characters should also have a paper cup.

4. As the sun shines on the bodies of water and the plants, they should one by one take a cup of water from their buckets and put it into one of the cloud buckets. After a person takes a cup of water to the clouds, he or she should squat down.

5. The wind should always be blowing gently so the clouds are moving slowly. When one of the clouds has a full bucket, it should begin to rain. In order to rain, the student cloud takes cups of water, one at a time, from the full bucket and puts them into the buckets of the bodies of water and plants that are below it. Whenever someone gets water, he or she should again stand. These students can then rejoin those adding water to the buckets of the clouds.

c. Using the information they have gained, have students construct a display of the water cycle on the bulletin board or on a transparency.

13. Letter to the Clean Water Foundation

a. Have several students draft a letter to the Clean Water Foundation for a packet of materials on the Clean Water Act. The packet will also include information on what the students can do to ensure clean water. Write to:

America's Clean Water Foundation
750 First Street, NE Suite 911
Washington DC 20002
202-898-0902

b. Ask several other students to read the draft letter to ensure that the request is clear. Have students revise and edit the letter before mailing it.

14. Survey on Home Water Use

a. To help students understand how water is used in many households, have each student complete the "Water Use" survey found on page 63. When the surveys are returned, have students compile and chart the results. Then hold a class meeting to study how the students and their families use water.

b. Have students use the resource materials listed in the bibliography to help find answers to the following questions.

How much water does it take to flush a toilet?

How much water is used to take a five-minute shower?

How much water does it take to run a dishwasher?

How much water does it take to wash a load of clothes?

15. Use of Water in the School

a. Have students count the number of toilets and faucets in the school. Discuss whether anyone has ever seen one of the faucets running when no one was using it.

b. Interview the cooks to find out how much water is generally used in preparing breakfast and lunch.

c. Interview the custodians to see how they use water and about how much water they use each day.

Air—It's What We Breathe

*T*he activities in this section are designed to expand the students' awareness of air pollution, the greenhouse effect and global warming, acid rain, the ozone, and what students can do to help reverse the effects of air pollution.

1. Interesting and Important Information to Know

Choose several of the following pieces of information to write on cards and then display the cards around the classroom. You also might have students form small groups to create posters based on the information.

- All the air around the Earth is called *the atmosphere*.

- Both oxygen and carbon dioxide are necessary for life.

- The natural greenhouse effect keeps the Earth at a comfortable average temperature of about 59° F.

- The energy from the sun is soaked up by the ocean and the land and then is reflected back. The ground level ozone and trace gases of carbon dioxide, methane, and nitrogen oxides in the atmosphere absorb some of this energy, keeping much of the heat close to the Earth. This process could cause the Earth to get uncomfortably warm.

- The burning of fossil fuels—coal, oil, and gas— is the greatest contributor of carbon dioxide in the atmosphere.

- Until the 1700's, the amount of carbon dioxide in the atmosphere was about 260 parts per million (ppm). After 1700, this number began to rise. In the 1960's the amount of carbon dioxide was about 315 ppm. In the last 30 years, the carbon dioxide level has risen to 350 ppm. The amount of carbon dioxide is increasing by approximately 1/2 percent per year.

- Factories and plants that burn coal and oil release about 1.5 billion tons of carbon dioxide into the air each year.

- Each gallon of gas burned in cars and trucks gives off between 5 and 6 pounds of carbon dioxide.

- There are about 400 million cars in the world.

- Acid rain occurs when sulfur dioxide and nitrogen oxide from the burning of fossil fuels mix with water.

- The issue of the ozone layer and ultraviolet radiation is still controversial. There are four long-term databases used to assess the Earth's ozone layer and all four provide limited and sometimes conflicting data. Many scientists feel that while we should be concerned about the future, there are still lots of unknowns and that we should guard against extreme reactions.

2. Testing the Air

a. Have students spread a very thin layer of petroleum jelly on coffee filters or 3" x 5" cards fastened to sticks of various lengths. Take pictures to compare filters or cards at the end of the experiment. Students should place the sticks or hang the filters or cards in various locations at their homes and around the school.

b. To test the air over a period of several days, students can put several filters at the same location and bring them in at different intervals. Be sure to have students label the locations, the various heights of the sticks, and the lengths of time the filters were in place.

c. Have students attach the filters or cards to a large chart, such as the one on page 49. Students should record on the chart the length of time the materials were outside and where they were located.

d. After the chart has been completed, ask students what they observed. Are the filters the same color as when they were put outside? What difference did the length of time outside make in the color of the filter or card? Take pictures of the filters or cards and compare them with pictures from the beginning of the experiment.

HOW CLEAN IS OUR AIR?

	school (near building)	school (in the open)	J's home (in tree)	R's home (backyard)
1 day				
3 days				
5 days				
7 days				
14 days				

e. Encourage students to raise questions about what they observed. What else would they like to know? Ask students whether they can see all the pollutants in the air or whether there might be some they cannot see.

f. Write each of the students' questions on separate sheets of paper and display them on a bulletin board. Challenge students to find the causes and effects of air pollution by reading the various books in the bibliography, by interviewing people, and through observations. As students come across information, they should jot the ideas down on a sticky note and attach it to the appropriate sheet. Discuss the students' findings.

3. Cars and Trucks and Air Pollution

a. Encourage each of the students to find a fairly busy intersection and count the number of cars that pass the intersection within a 30-minute time period.

b. Using the information in the "Important and Interesting Information to Know" activity found on pages 47 and 48, have students determine how many pounds of carbon dioxide could be released into the air within a 30-minute time period, assuming each car used 1 gallon of gas.

c. Have students determine the total amount of carbon dioxide that could be released when they combine the totals for all the intersections observed.

d. Encourage each student to find out the average number of gallons of gas the members of his or her family uses each week. Ask students to determine the approximate number of pounds of carbon dioxide that could be released during one week from the cars of his or her family members.

e. Invite a car mechanic to come speak to the class about how the emission of gases is regulated.

f. In a group discussion, raise the following questions:

Should we reduce our dependence on motor vehicles? Why or why not?

How can we reduce our dependence on cars and trucks?

What is needed in the community to reduce our dependence on motor vehicles?

4. Carbon Dioxide and the Burning of Fossil Fuels

Write the question "What are 'fossil' fuels?" on the chalkboard. By reading the books and magazines that are in the classroom, challenge students to find out what fossil fuels are, who uses them, and why they are used. When the students have found the information they need, hold a class meeting to discuss their findings.

5. Methane, Nitrogen Oxides, Ground-Level Ozone

Challenge students to look through a variety of resource materials to find out how methane and nitrous oxide gases are formed and how they are related to the everyday activities of people. Discuss the effect of these gases on the environment.

6. Traveling Pollution

Demonstrate for students how the smell of perfume travels by spraying a small amount of perfume into the air. Then pose the following problem to the students:

> Suppose an area of a state has a very high level of carbon dioxide and ground-level ozone. In another part of the state, 200 miles away, the people are very concerned about this pollution and want the people in the area with the pollution to do something about it. Should the people 200 miles away be concerned? If yes, why? If no, why not?

7. The Greenhouse Effect

If students have not mentioned that the gases they have been researching contribute to the greenhouse effect, introduce the concept. Explain that carbon dioxide, methane, and nitrous oxide absorb the long-wave, invisible radiation from the sun, rather than allowing the heat to be radiated away from the Earth, much like glass absorbs radiation in a greenhouse. This, in the opinion of some scientists, threatens to change weather patterns, cause the extinction of many species of plants and animals, and greatly change the Earth's land use. You can create the greenhouse effect with the following experiment.

You will need the following materials:

> small empty fish tank or clear glass bowl
>
> 2 thermometers
>
> 2 sheets of plastic wrap, large enough to lap over all four edges of the glass bowl (one of the plastic sheets should have several small holes punched in it)
>
> masking tape

Procedure:

1. Place the thermometer in the glass bowl and record the temperature. Keep a record of the temperature outside the bowl as well.

2. After a few hours, read the temperature. Record the time and the temperature again.

3. Cover the bowl or fish tank with the plastic wrap with holes. Tape down each of the sides. After a few hours, have students record the time and the temperature again. What are the students' observations about the temperature in the bowl?

4. Cover the bowl with the second sheet of plastic wrap and tape down the edges. After a few hours, have students read and record the temperature. What do the students think is contributing to the rise in temperature? Ask students what this experiment explains about the greenhouse effect.

8. Global Warming

a. Help students explore what effect trace gases have on global warming by sharing newspaper and magazine articles on the subject. Remind the students that the greenhouse effect is essential to life because it prevents extreme hot or cold temperatures.

b. Ask students to read the materials very carefully to determine whether the negative effects of the greenhouse effect are a certainty or whether scientists are predicting what they think might happen. Ask students to cite their evidence on the basis of the information in the resources provided on pages 12–15. Discuss what makes it difficult to predict what will happen in the future.

9. Experiment with the Effect of Acids on Plants

Inform students that a number of trees and other plants are dying each year because of acid pollutants in the rain. This is called *acid rain*. Have students list in a column everything they know about acid rain. Then encourage students to raise questions. List the questions in a second column. Have small groups try to find answers to the questions. In conjunction, run the following experiment.

You will need the following materials:

> 2 plants of the same kind and about the same size
>
> several teaspoons of lemon juice
>
> litmus paper and color strip

Procedure:

1. Show students the two plants. Encourage students to predict what would happen if a few teaspoons of lemon juice were added to the water used for watering one of the plants. Water one of the plants with lemon-juice water. Label the plant.

2. Place the plants in a lighted area and water each plant once a week. Add two teaspoons of lemon juice to the water for the labeled plant. Test the acidity of the lemon juice/water combination by putting a litmus tab in a small amount of lemon-juice water for 24 hours. Compare the litmus tab to the color strip on page 38. Take pictures of both plants throughout the experiment.

3. Encourage students to chart the dates the plants were watered and their appearance at each watering. Stop using the lemon-juice water once visible signs of the plant's poor health appear.

4. Ask students to speculate why the plant watered with the lemon juice is doing poorly.

10. Experiment to Determine Amount of Acidity in Rain in Local Areas

You will need the following materials:

    1 pail, washed and dried

    litmus paper and color strip

    bottled water

Procedure:

1. Collect rain in a clean pail.

2. Pour enough bottled water into a glass dish to cover a litmus tab. Pour enough rain water into another dish to cover a litmus tab. Leave the litmus tabs in the two containers for 24 hours.

3. Encourage students to observe and record what happened. How acidic is the bottled water? The rain water? Compare the acidity of the rain water with the acidity of the water samples tested earlier.

11. Miming the Formation of the Ozone Layer

Ask students to locate in one of the resource books information about the importance of the ozone layer. Help students understand the formation of the ozone through the following mime.

Characters:

    sun

    several ultraviolet rays

    several oxygen molecules
       (2 students holding hands)

    several ozone molecules
       (3 students holding hands in a circle)

Narration:

1. The sun shines. (Sun should shine on all the molecules.)

2. Ultraviolet rays coming from the sun split the oxygen molecules into two oxygen atoms, which float free. (The ultraviolet rays make the two atoms of the oxygen molecules let go of hands and float freely about the room.)

3. The free oxygen atoms hook up with oxygen molecules to form ozone molecules. (Form groups of 3 oxygen atoms.)

12. Miming the Destruction of the Ozone Layer

a. Explain that the sun's ultraviolet rays break up more oxygen atoms from the ozone molecules than from the oxygen molecules because it's easier. When an oxygen atom breaks off from an ozone molecule, it floats free and often hooks up with another oxygen molecule to form an ozone molecule, or it hooks up with another existing oxygen atom to form an oxygen molecule.

b. Inform students that chlorofluorocarbons (CFCs) can also break up ozone molecules. Point out that CFCs are found in refrigerators, air conditioners, and all Styrofoam used in cups and fast-food boxes. Explain that CFCs can destroy ozone. Mime the break-up of ozone by CFCs.

Characters:

sun

chlorofluorocarbons (compounds of methane, fluorine, chlorine) (3 or 4 groups of 1 atom of methane, 1 of fluorine, and 1 of chlorine— 3 students link arms)

ozone molecules (remainder of class are ozone molecules—3 students holding hands in a circle)

Narration:

1. The sun's radiation breaks the chlorofluorocarbons apart releasing the atoms. (The sun makes the three atoms in the chlorofluorocarbons let go of hands and float freely about the room.)

2. The chlorine (C) atoms interact with ozone molecules, pulling away the third atom—which converts ozone molecules back into oxygen molecules. One chlorine atom can destroy 100,000 ozone molecules. (Each chlorine atom pulls one of the three atoms in the ozone molecule away from the other two—the remaining oxygen atoms hold hands and float around the room as an oxygen molecule.)

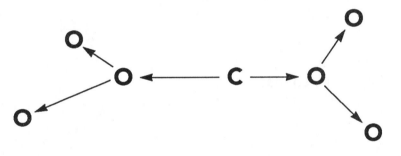

13. What Can Be Done About Pollution?

a. Give students a copy of the chart "What Can Be Done About Pollution" found on page 64. Have the students ask people outside of school for their opinions on what can be done about air pollution.

b. Form cooperative working groups to compile the responses into a new chart. Have groups include any new ideas that come up as they are working. Have each group share its ideas with the class. Record the ideas on a large sheet of butcher paper. As a group, read over the list. Encourage students to share their thoughts about any of the ideas presented.

14. Writing an Essay or Letter

a. Ask students to reread their notes and any charts displayed in the classroom. Suggest that students take one environmental issue and decide what their positions are on that issue. Have students record any relevant facts.

b. Encourage students to write a persuasive essay or letter to someone in school, a friend, a parent, or someone in the local government. They should include a statement about the issue they have chosen, pertinent facts, their opinions, and reasons for their opinions.

c. Suggest that students share their rough drafts with several classmates. Authors should ask the reviewers to share their reactions on how well the issue is stated and how persuasive the letter is. Authors should then make the needed changes.

d. Publish the essays in an environmental newsletter. After the letters have been edited and recopied, mail them for the students.

15. Environmental Newsletter

a. Ask students to review all the articles, editorials, and cartoons that they have written or drawn. Have each student select one piece that he or she would like to contribute to the newsletter.

b. During the selections, look for a balance in the information presented. Ask for volunteers to write needed articles or draw additional cartoons.

c. Select students to help finish the paper. Make copies of the newsletter for the students, the principal, and the media center. You may wish to send the newsletter to community leaders, as well.

16. Class Book on the Environment

a. Have students look at all the pictures that have been taken during this unit and categorize them into appropriate groupings.

b. Divide the class into small groups. Give each group a cluster of pictures and paper to make a booklet. Ask groups to decide how the pictures should be arranged and to write appropriate captions beneath the photographs.

c. Decide which articles, editorials, letters, and cartoons should be included.

d. Combine the pages together into a book. Have the students decide on a title. Include each student's name as one of the authors.

17. Debates

a. Encourage students to debate the following issues:

Topic 1: Our need to burn fossil fuels for energy outweighs the negative effects of pollution.

Topic 2: It is more important to use fertilizers to raise more crops to feed a growing number of people than it is to be concerned about the effect of fertilizers on the environment.

Topic 3: I'm only one person and one person can't make much of a difference in stopping pollution.

Topic 4: Global warming is not a real threat.

b. Have students draw topics out of a hat. Draw, too, whether they are supposed to argue in favor of the topic or against it.

c. Have students review all the data from the surveys, the charts, and the materials they read and wrote about while preparing for the debate. The teams should decide who will be the first speaker and who will respond to the opposite team. Assist the teams as needed.

d. Each team is to have two to three minutes for each speaker.

e. Invite several teachers to serve as judges. Ask that the feedback to the teams include what they did well, as well as how they could have strengthened their points.

Name _____

Our Way of Life Survey

Directions: Read each of the statements and circle *yes* or *no*.

1. Yes   No   Have you ever eaten at a fast-food restaurant and been served food in a plastic or Styrofoam carton?

2. Yes   No   Has someone in your family brought home groceries in a plastic or paper bag?

3. Yes   No   Within the last week, have you written on only one side of a sheet of paper and then thrown the sheet away?

4. Yes   No   Have you ridden in a car during the last three days?
                If so, how many times?

5. Yes   No   Have you ridden in a car when you could have walked or taken a bike?

6. Yes   No   Have you or any one in your family thrown any glass or plastic bottles into the garbage?

7. Yes   No   Have you or any one in your family thrown newspapers into the garbage?

Name _____

Kinds and Amounts of Trash at Home

Directions: **1.** Weigh each wastebasket or garbage pail in your home on a bathroom scale. (Weigh the wastebasket or garbage pail empty.) **2.** For one week, weigh each wastebasket and garbage pail whenever full of trash. Subtract the weight of the wastebasket or pail to find out the weight of the trash. **3.** Sort the trash into newspapers, magazines, other kinds of paper, plastic bottles and containers, and glass bottles. Weigh each bag of items and write the weights in the space provided on the chart below. Wear gloves when sorting trash.

Date	Weight of Trash	Newspapers	Magazines	Other Paper	Plastic	Glass
Total Weight of Trash for the Week						

For Your Information: The average American throws out 3 1/2 to 4 pounds of trash per day. Divide the total weight of your family's trash by the number of people in your family. How does your family compare to the average? Share the results with your family.

Water Use Survey

Directions: Share this survey with the members of your family. Tell them that you are studying the environment and how people use water. Take this survey back to school in two days. As a class, we will be looking at how people use water and ways in which water might be conserved. Please do not put your name on this survey.

Never Sometimes Usually

1   2   3   One or more faucets drip.

1   2   3   Water runs while we brush our teeth.

1   2   3   We run the dishwasher with small loads.

1   2   3   We run the washing machine with small loads.

1   2   3   In summer, we wash the car at least once a week.

1   2   3   In summer, we water the grass about once a week.

1   2   3   We use the garbage disposal to get rid of scraps of food.

List other ways your family uses water in a week's time.

1   2   3   _____

1   2   3   _____

1   2   3   _____

Name _____

What Can Be Done About Pollution?

Directions: Talk to people in your family or in your neighborhood about pollution. Ask how they would answer the questions that follow. After all the reading and talking you have done with your classmates, think about what might be done about water, air, or land pollution. Be creative. Write down your answers. Share your favorite ideas with your classmates.

What Can Be Done About _____ Pollution?

Who can take action?	What might be done?
new inventions	
new laws	
groups of people	
individuals	
What will you do?	